Whistler V. Ruskin: Art & Art Critics

James Abbot McN. Whistler

Whistler v. Ruskin

ART & ART CRITICS

J. A. McN. WHISTLER

The White House, Chelsea

Dec. 24, 1878

Whistler v. Ruskin

ART & ART CRITICS

BY

J. A. MacNEILL WHISTLER

Fourth Edition

London

CHATTO & WINDUS, PICCADILLY.

LONDON: PRINTED BY

SPOTTISWOODE AND CO., NEW-STREET SQUARE

AND PARLIAMENT STREET

DEDICATED

TO

ALBERT MOORE

\

WHISTLER v. *RUSKIN*.

THE *fin mot* and spirit of this matter seems
to have been utterly missed, or perhaps
willingly winked at, by the journals in their
comments. Their correspondents have per-
sistently, and not unnaturally as writers, seen
nothing beyond the immediate case in law, viz.,
the difference between Mr. Ruskin and myself, culminating in the libel with a verdict for
the plaintiff.

Now the war, of which the opening skirmish
was fought the other day in Westminster, is
really one between the Brush and the Pen ; and
involves literally, as the Attorney-General himself hinted, the absolute *raison d'être* of the
critic. The cry, on their part, of ' Il faut vivre,'

I most certainly meèt, in this case, with the appropriate answer, 'Je n'en vois pas la nécessité.'

Far from me, at that stage of things, to go further into this discussion than I did, when, cross-examined by Sir John Holker, I contented myself with the general answer, 'that one might admit criticism when emanating from a man who had passed his whole life in the science which he attacks.' The position of Mr. Ruskin as an art-authority we left quite unassailed during the trial. To have said that Mr. Ruskin's pose among intelligent men, as other than a *littérateur*, is false and ridiculous, would have been an invitation to the stake ; and to be burnt alive, or stoned before the verdict, was not what I came into court for.

Over and over again did the Attorney-General cry out aloud, in the agony of his cause, 'What is to become of painting if the critics withhold their lash ?' As well might he ask what is to become of mathematics under similar circumstances were they possible. I maintain that two and two the mathematician would continue to make four, in spite of the whine of the amateur for three, or the cry of the critic for five. We are told that Mr. Ruskin has devoted his long life to art, and as a result—is Slade Professor at Oxford. In the same sentence, we have thus his position and its worth. It suffices not, Messieurs! a life passed among pictures makes not a painter—else the policeman in the National Gallery might assert himself. As well allege that he who lives in a library must needs die a poet. Let not Mr. Ruskin flatter himself that more education makes the difference between himself and the policeman when both stand gazing in the Gallery!

There they might remain till the end of time; the one decently silent, the other saying, in good English, many high-sounding empty things, like the crackling of thorns under a pot —undismayed by the presence of the Masters, with whose names he is sacrilegiously familiar; whose intentions he interprets, whose vices he discovers with the facility of the incapable, and whose virtues he descants upon with a verbosity and flow of language that would, could he hear it, give Titian the same shock of surprise that was Balaam's, when the first great critic proffered his opinion.

This one instance apart, where collapse was immediate, the creature Critic is of comparatively modern growth—and certainly, in perfect condition, of recent date. To his completeness go qualities evolved from the latest lightnesses of to-day—indeed, the *fine fleur* of his type is brought forth in Paris, and beside him the Englishman is but rough-hewn and blundering after all ; though not unkindly should one say it, as reproaching him with inferiority resulting from chances neglected. The truth is, as compared with his brother of the Boulevards, the Briton was badly begun by nature. To take himself seriously is the fate of the humbug at Home, and destruction to the jaunty career of the art critic, whose essence of success lies in his strong sense of his ephemeral existence, and his consequent horror of *ennuyer*'ing his world—in short, to perceive the joke of life is rarely given to our people, whilst it forms the mainspring of the Parisian's *savoir plaire*. The *finesse* of the Frenchman, acquired in long loafing and clever café cackle—the glib go and easy assurance of the *petit crevé*, combined with the *chic* of great habit—the brilliant *blague* of the ateliers—the aptitude of their *argot*—the fling of the *Figaro*, and the knack of short paragraphs, which allows him to print of a picture, 'C'est bien écrit!' and of a subject, 'C'est bien dit!'—these are elements of an *ensemble* impossible in this Island.

Still, we are 'various' in our specimens, and a sense of progress is noticeable when we look about among them. Indications of their period are perceptible, and curiously enough a similarity is suggested, by their work, between themselves and the vehicles we might fancy carrying them about to their livelihood.

Tough old Tom, the busy City 'Bus, with its heavy jolting and many halts ; its steady, sturdy, stodgy continuance on the same old much-worn way, every turning known, and freshness un-hoped for ; its patient dreary dulness of daily duty to its cheap company—struggling on to its end, nevertheless, and pulling up at the Bank ! with a flourish from the driver, and a joke from the cad at the door. Then the contributors to the daily papers : so many hansoms bowling along that the moment may not be lost, and the *àpropos* gone for ever. The one or two broughams solemnly rolling for Reviews, while the lighter bicycle zigzags irresponsibly in among them for the happy Halfpennies.

What a commerce it all is, to be sure !

No sham in it either !—no 'bigod nonsense !' they are all 'doing good'—yes, they all do good to Art. Poor Art ! what a sad state the slut is in, an these gentlemen shall help her. The artist alone, by the way, is to no purpose, and remains unconsulted ; his work is explained and rectified without him, by the one who was never in it—but upon whom God, always good, though sometimes careless, has thrown away the knowledge refused to the author—poor devil !

The Attorney-General said, 'There are some people who would do away with critics altogether.' I agree with him, and am of the irrationals he points at—but let me be clearly understood—the *art* critic alone would I extinguish. That writers should destroy writings to the benefit of writing is reasonable. Who but they shall insist upon beauties of literature, and discard the demerits of their brother *littérateurs?* In their turn they will be destroyed by other writers, and the merry game goes on till truth prevail. Shall the painter then—I foresee the question—decide upon painting ? Shall *he* be the critic and sole authority ? Aggressive as is this supposition, I fear that, in the length of time, his assertion alone has established what even the gentlemen of the quill accept as the

canons of art, and recognise as the masterpieces
of work.

Let work, then, be received in silence, as it
was in the days to which the penmen still point
as an era when art was at its apogee. And
here we come upon the oft-repeated apology of
the critic for existing at all, and find how com-
plete is his stultification.   He brands himself as
the necessary blister for the health of the painter,
and writes that he may do good to his art.   In
the same ink he bemoans the decadence about
him, and declares that the best work was done
when he was not there to help it.   No! let
there be no critics! they are not a 'necessary
evil,' but an evil quite unnecessary, though an
evil certainly.   Harm they do, and not good.
Furnished as they are with the means of fur-
thering their foolishness, they spread prejudice
abroad ; and through the papers, at their service,
thousands are warned against the work they
have yet to look upon.   And here one is tempted
to go further, and show the crass idiocy and

impertinence of those whose *dicta* are printed as law.

How he of the *Times*[1] has found Velasquez 'slovenly in execution, poor in colour—being little but a combination of neutral greys and ugly in its forms'—how he grovelled in happiness over a Turner—that was no Turner at all, as Mr. Ruskin wrote to show—Ruskin! whom he has since defended. Ah! Messieurs, what our neighbours call *la malice des choses* was unthought of, and the sarcasm of fate was against you. How Gerard Dow's broom was an example for the young; and Canaletti and Paul Veronese are to be swept aside—doubtless with it. How Rembrandt is coarse, and Carlo Dolci noble—with more of this kind. But what does it matter! 'What does anything matter!' The farce will go on, and its solemnity adds to the fun.

Mediocrity flattered at acknowledging mediocrity, and mistaking mystification for mastery,

[1] *Times*, June 6, 1864.

enters the fog of dilettantism, and, graduating connoisseur, ends its days in a bewilderment of *bric-à-brac* and Brummagem!

'Taste' has long been confounded with capacity, and accepted as sufficient qualification for the utterance of judgment in music, poetry, and painting. Art is joyously received as a matter of opinion; and that it should be based upon laws as rigid and defined as those of the known sciences, is a supposition no longer to be tolerated by modern cultivation. For whereas no polished member of society is at all affected at admitting himself neither engineer, mathematician, nor astronomer, and therefore remains willingly discreet and taciturn upon these subjects, still would he be highly offended were he supposed to have no voice in what is clearly to him a matter of 'taste'; and so he becomes of necessity the backer of the critic —the cause and result of his own ignorance and vanity! The fascination of this pose is too much for him, and he hails with delight its justification. Modesty and good sense are revolted at nothing, and the millennium of 'Taste' sets in.

The whole scheme is simple : the galleries are to be thrown open on Sundays, and the public, dragged from their beer to the British Museum, are to delight in the Elgin Marbles, and appreciate what the Early Italians have done to elevate their thirsty souls! An inroad into the laboratory would be looked upon as an intrusion ; but before the triumphs of art, the expounder is at his ease, and points out the doctrine that Raphael's results are within the reach of any beholder, provided he enroll himself with Ruskin or hearken to Colvin in the provinces. The people are to be educated upon the broad basis of 'taste,' forsooth, and it matters but little what 'gentleman and scholar' undertake the task. Eloquence alone shall guide them—and the readiest writer or wordiest talker is perforce their professor.

The Observatory at Greenwich under the direction of an apothecary! the College of

Physicians with Tennyson as President! and we know that madness is about. But a school of art with an accomplished *littérateur* at its head disturbs no one! and is actually what the world receives as rational, while Ruskin writes for pupils and Colvin holds forth at Cambridge.

Still, quite alone stands Ruskin, whose writing is art, and whose art is unworthy his writing. To him and his example do we owe the outrage of proffered assistance from the unscientific—the meddling of the immodest—the intrusion of the garrulous. Art, that for ages has hewn its own history in marble, and written its own comments on canvas, shall it suddenly stand still, and stammer, and wait for wisdom from the passer-by?—for guidance from the hand that holds neither brush nor chisel? Out upon the shallow conceit! What greater sarcasm can Mr. Ruskin pass upon himself than that he preaches to young men what he cannot perform! Why, unsatisfied with his conscious power, should he choose to become the type of incompetence by talking for forty years of what he has never done !

Let him resign his present professorship, to fill the Chair of Ethics at the University. As Master of English Literature he has a right to his laurels, while as the Populariser of Pictures he remains the Peter Parley of Painting.

CPSIA information can be obtained at www.ICGtesting.com
Printed in the USA
LVOW02s2105010414

379826LV00011B/534/P